PICTURE THIS
HUMAN
BODY

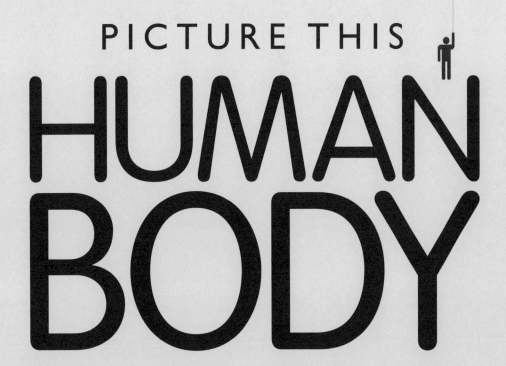

KINGFISHER
LONDON & NEW YORK

Copyright © Kingfisher 2013
Published in the United States by Kingfisher,
175 Fifth Ave., New York, NY 10010
Kingfisher is an imprint of Macmillan Children's Books, London.
All rights reserved.

Author: Margaret Hynes
Illustrations: Andy Crisp
Consultant: Dr. Patricia Macnair
Designer: Jack Clucas
Developed by: Simon Holland

With special thanks to Peter Winfield

Distributed in the U.S. and Canada by Macmillan, 175 Fifth Ave., New York, NY 10010

Library of Congress Cataloging-in-Publication data has been applied for.

ISBN: 978-0-7534-6888-3

Kingfisher books are available for special promotions and premiums.
For details contact: Special Markets Department, Macmillan, 175 Fifth Ave., New York, NY 10010.

For more information, please visit www.kingfisherbooks.com

1 3 5 7 9 8 6 4 2
1TR/0213/UTD/WKT/140WF
Printed in China

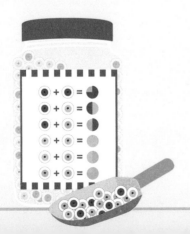

PICTURE THIS
HUMAN BODY

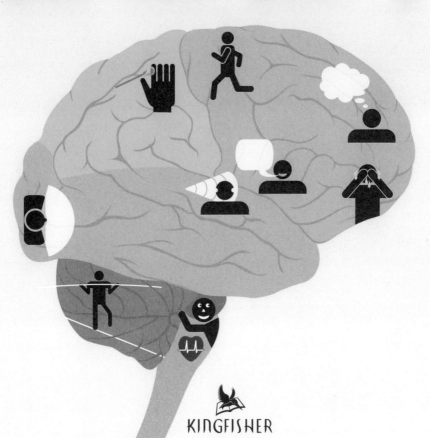

KINGFISHER
NEW YORK

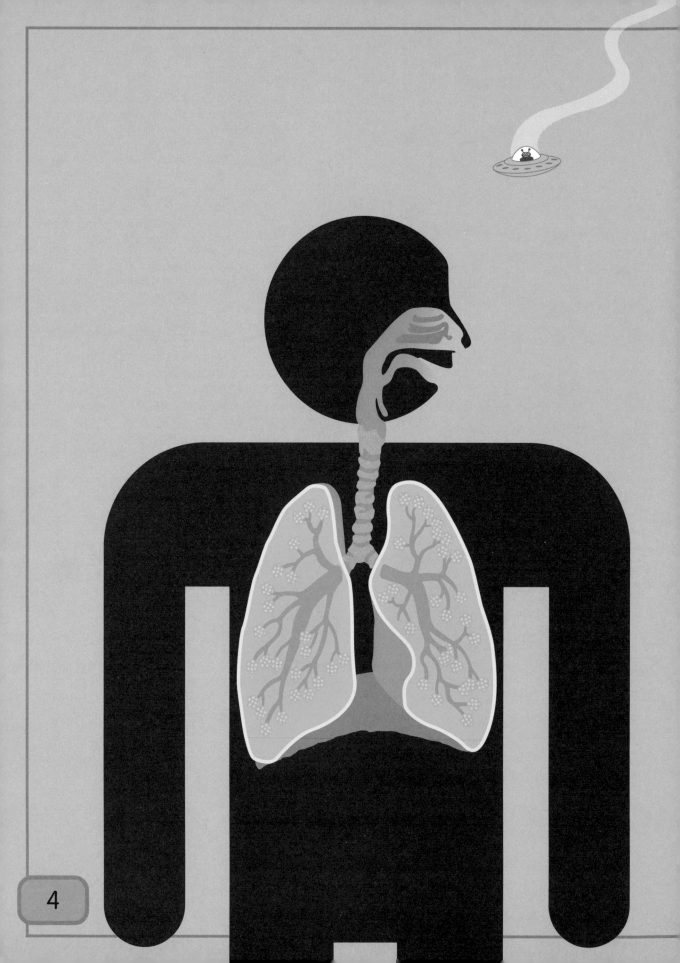

Contents

Magnificent measures

This book is bursting with information graphics, or pictures, that illustrate facts and figures relating to the human body. Any measurements are shown using the U.S. Customary system, which describes length in feet, volume in pints or gallons, and weight in pounds. If you use meters, liters, and kilograms instead, you are using the metric system (in parentheses). The graphics on these pages compare the two amounts and will help you visualize the units.

Speed

Mph is a unit of speed, expressing the number of miles traveled in one hour. This speedometer shows how mph compares with kilometers per hour (km/h).

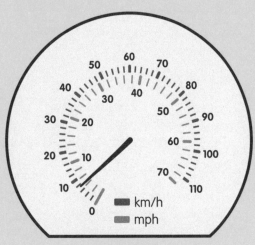

Volume

This pitcher holds 35 fluid ounces (35 fl. oz.), or just over 2 pints. This is equal to 1,000 milliliters, or 1 liter.

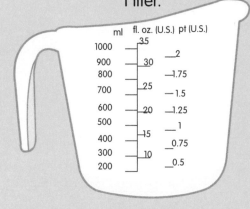

Distance

HIGHWAY 50

Newtown 0.6 mi. (1km)

Townsville 6 mi. (10km)

Length
There are 12 inches (12 in.) in a foot. There are also ten millimeters (10mm) in one centimeter (1cm), 100 centimeters in one meter (1m), and 1,000 meters in one kilometer (1km). This ruler shows centimeters (cm) and inches (in.).

Weight

Sixteen ounces (16 oz.) equal one pound (1 lb.), and 2,000 pounds (2,000 lb.) equal one ton. In metric, 1,000g equal 1kg, and 1,000kg equal one metric tonne (1t).

Paperclip

0.035 oz. (1g)

Coconut

2 lb. (0.91kg)

Small car

1 ton (0.91t)

Temperature

Celsius (metric)

Fahrenheit (Customary)

5 ft. (1.52m)

9 ft. (2.74m)

11 square feet (1 square meter)

Area

This is calculated by multiplying the length of an area by its width. Here you can see what one square meter looks like when compared with the area of a Ping-Pong table.

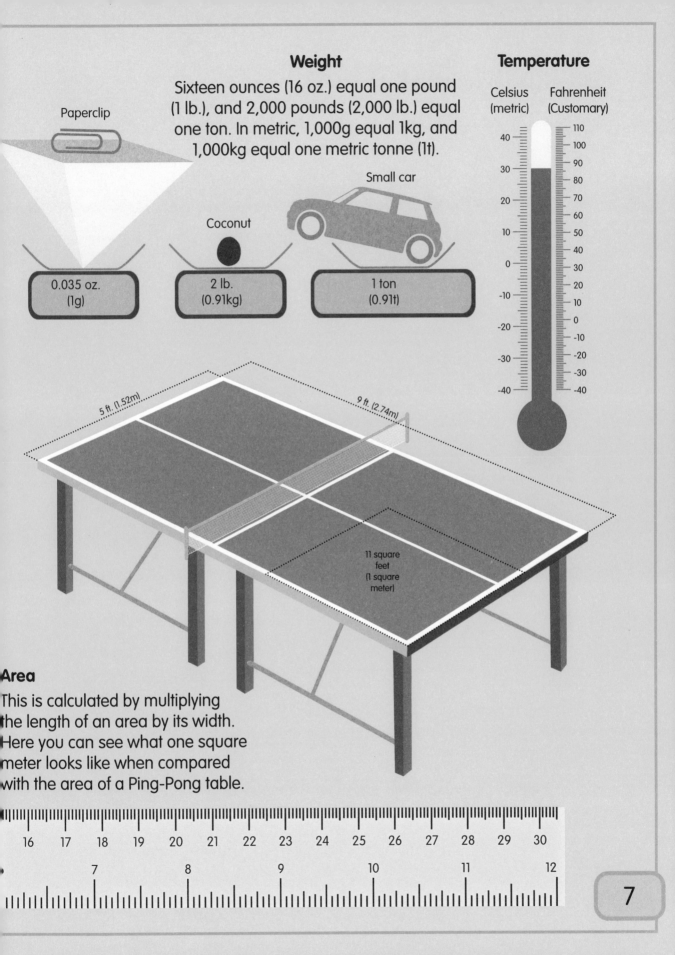

Building blocks

You are built from billions of microscopic living structures called cells. There are more than 200 different types of human cells, each of which performs different tasks. For example, sperm cells and egg cells fuse together to make babies, red blood cells carry oxygen around your body, and skin cells make up your outer layer. Cells of the same type may be organized together into tissue. Many tissues combine to form an organ, such as the stomach. Several organs work together in an organ system.

Body building

Cell

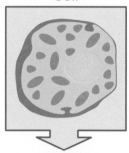

Tissue

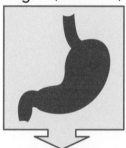

Organ (stomach)

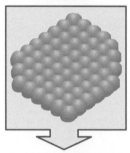

Organ system (digestive)

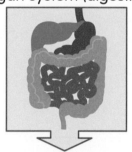

Organism (human man)

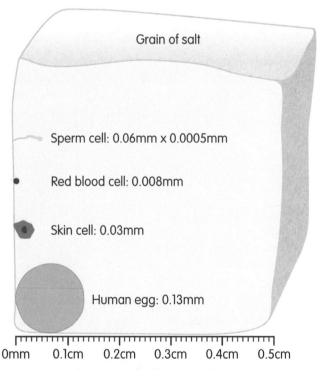

Grain of salt

Sperm cell: 0.06mm x 0.0005mm

Red blood cell: 0.008mm

Skin cell: 0.03mm

Human egg: 0.13mm

0mm   0.1cm   0.2cm   0.3cm   0.4cm   0.5cm

Microscopic living things

To get an idea of the size of cells, here are some compared with a grain of salt. Millimeters are used because the scale is so small.

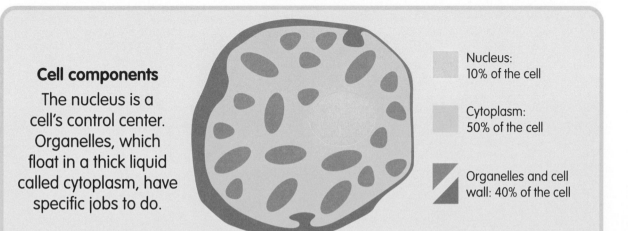

Cell components

The nucleus is a cell's control center. Organelles, which float in a thick liquid called cytoplasm, have specific jobs to do.

Nucleus:
10% of the cell

Cytoplasm:
50% of the cell

Organelles and cell wall: 40% of the cell

Lifespan of cells

Like all living things, cells die, though some live longer than others.

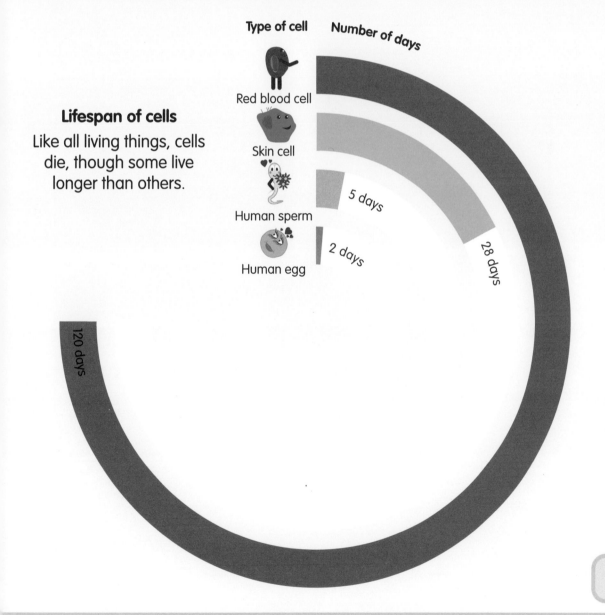

Type of cell

Number of days

Red blood cell

Skin cell

Human sperm

Human egg

5 days

2 days

28 days

120 days

Saliva per day

2% electrolytes, mucus, antibacterial compounds, and enzymes........

Saliva injector

98% water.........

3 pt. (1.5L)
2 pt. (1L)
1 pt. (0.5L)

Gastric juices per day

0.5% salt, hydrochloric acid, and enzymes........

99.5% water........

3 pt. (1.5L)
2 pt. (1L)
1 pt. (0.5L)

Esophagus
Food chute

Tongue
Taster and conveyor

`1:00:00`

Food approaching the mouth . . .

Mouth machine
Mechanical and chemical digester

`1:01:00`

In mouth: up to 1 minute

1 million glands........

`1:01:05`

In esophagus: 5–10 seconds

Stomach
Acid bath and mechanical pummel

`4:01:05`

In stomach: 3 hours

Food processing

Food is broken down into nutrients and waste as it works its way through a processing system known as the digestive system. The food is broken down mechanically by the teeth, which mash it into smaller pieces, and muscles in the stomach, which pummel it into a thick soup. Chemicals made by glands in the mouth, stomach, pancreas, liver, and small intestine break down the food even more so that it can be absorbed into the bloodstream and carried to the cells in the body.

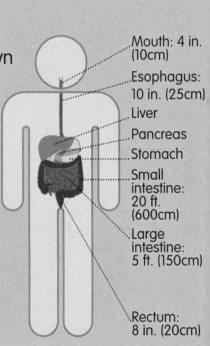

Mouth: 4 in. (10cm)

Esophagus: 10 in. (25cm)

Liver

Pancreas

Stomach

Small intestine: 20 ft. (600cm)

Large intestine: 5 ft. (150cm)

Rectum: 8 in. (20cm)

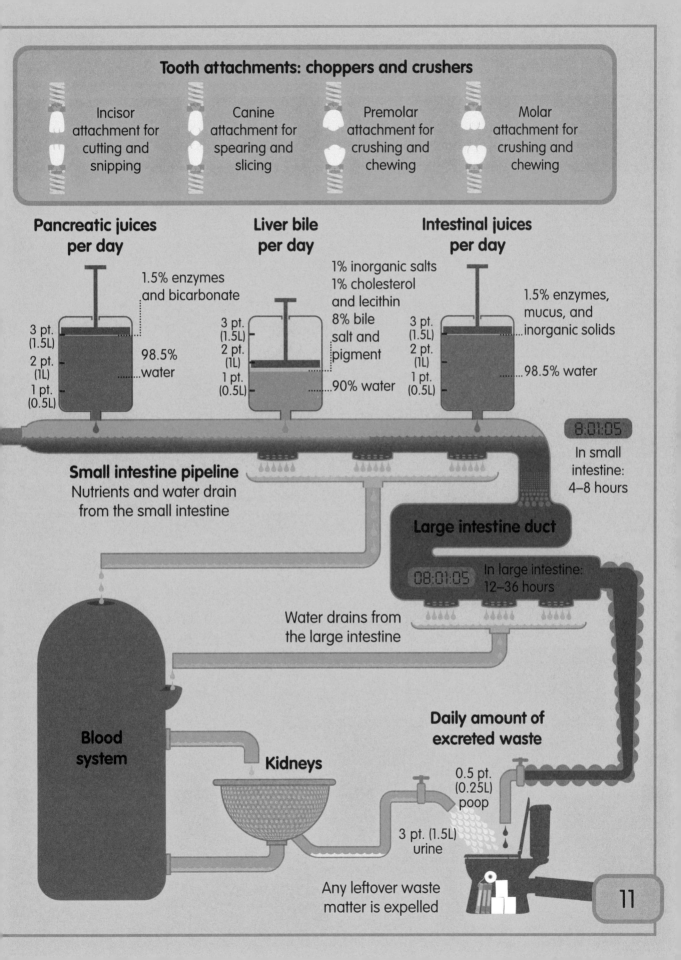

Tooth attachments: choppers and crushers

Incisor attachment for cutting and snipping

Canine attachment for spearing and slicing

Premolar attachment for crushing and chewing

Molar attachment for crushing and chewing

Pancreatic juices per day

1.5% enzymes and bicarbonate

3 pt. (1.5L)
2 pt. (1L)
1 pt. (0.5L)

98.5% water

Liver bile per day

1% inorganic salts
1% cholesterol and lecithin
8% bile salt and pigment

3 pt. (1.5L)
2 pt. (1L)
1 pt. (0.5L)

90% water

Intestinal juices per day

1.5% enzymes, mucus, and inorganic solids

3 pt. (1.5L)
2 pt. (1L)
1 pt. (0.5L)

98.5% water

8:01:05

In small intestine: 4–8 hours

Small intestine pipeline
Nutrients and water drain from the small intestine

Large intestine duct

08:01:05 In large intestine: 12–36 hours

Water drains from the large intestine

Blood system

Kidneys

Daily amount of excreted waste

0.5 pt. (0.25L) poop

3 pt. (1.5L) urine

Any leftover waste matter is expelled

11

Fueling the body

Food is the body's fuel. Parts of this fuel, called nutrients, help the body grow and repair itself and provide the energy the body needs to power its activities. The amount of fuel your body needs depends on what you do. For example, if you stayed in bed all day, your body would need very little energy. Scientists usually measure the energy we get from food in units called calories.

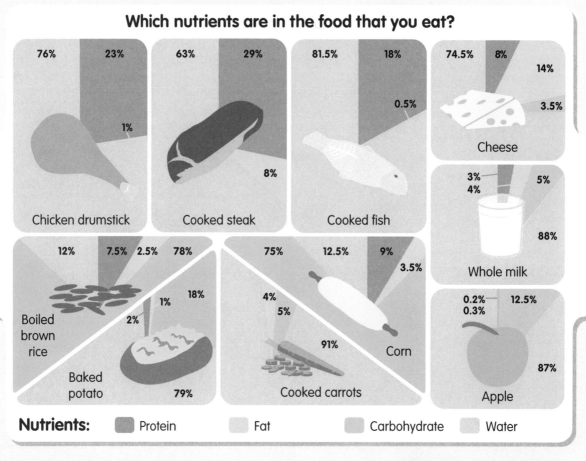

Which nutrients are in the food that you eat?

Chicken drumstick — 76%, 23%, 1%

Cooked steak — 63%, 29%, 8%

Cooked fish — 81.5%, 18%, 0.5%

Cheese — 74.5%, 8%, 14%, 3.5%

Whole milk — 3%, 4%, 5%, 88%

Boiled brown rice — 12%, 7.5%, 2.5%, 78%

Baked potato — 1%, 2%, 18%, 79%

Cooked carrots — 75%, 12.5%, 9%, 3.5%, 4%, 5%, 91%

Corn

Apple — 0.2%, 0.3%, 12.5%, 87%

Nutrients: ■ Protein ■ Fat ■ Carbohydrate ■ Water

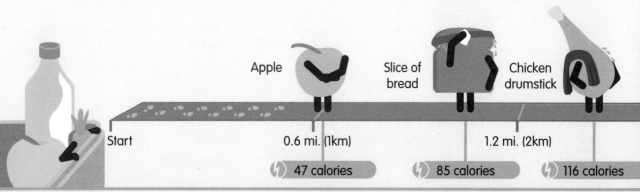

Start

Apple — 0.6 mi. (1km) — 47 calories

Slice of bread — 1.2 mi. (2km) — 85 calories

Chicken drumstick — 116 calories

Calorie counting

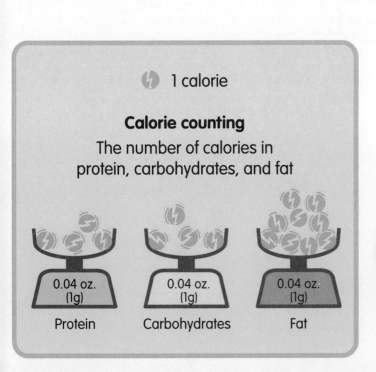

🔋 1 calorie

Calorie counting

The number of calories in protein, carbohydrates, and fat

0.04 oz. (1g)	0.04 oz. (1g)	0.04 oz. (1g)
Protein	Carbohydrates	Fat

13,210 gallons (50,000 liters) of liquid

110,230 lb. (50,000kg) of food

A lifetime supply of food and drink for a human

Calories burned each hour

Sleeping

75 calories

Watching TV

100 calories

Swimming

200 calories

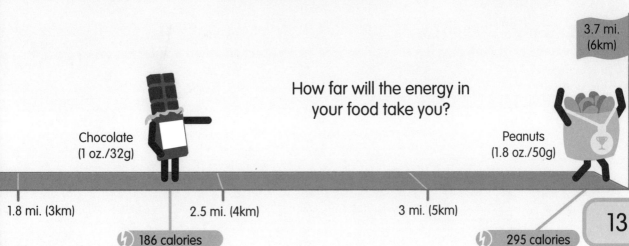

How far will the energy in your food take you?

Chocolate (1 oz./32g)

Peanuts (1.8 oz./50g)

3.7 mi. (6km)

1.8 mi. (3km)

2.5 mi. (4km)

3 mi. (5km)

🔋 186 calories

🔋 295 calories

Lungs in action

The cells in your body use oxygen from the air around you to release the energy stored in the food you eat. A poisonous waste called carbon dioxide is produced during this process. When you breathe in, air travels through a series of tubes to tiny air bags, called alveoli, in your lungs. It is here that the oxygen is taken from the air and passed on to the cells around your body, and carbon dioxide moves in the opposite direction to be breathed out.

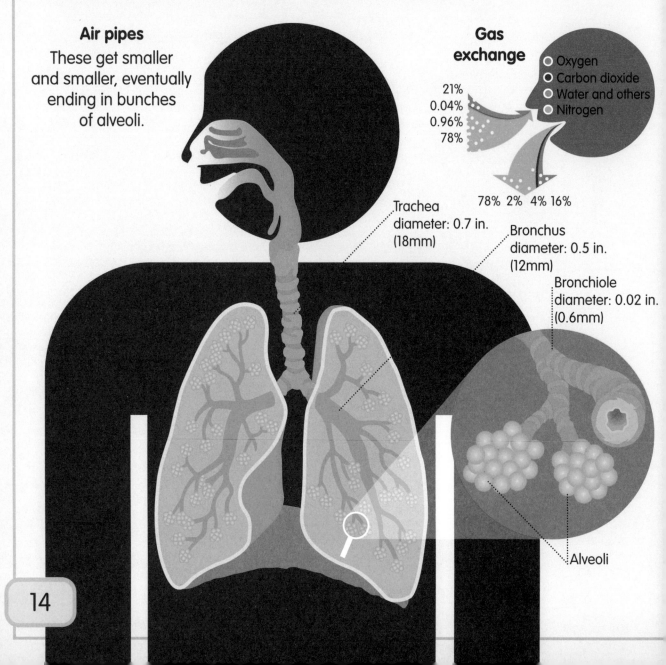

Air pipes
These get smaller and smaller, eventually ending in bunches of alveoli.

Gas exchange

- Oxygen
- Carbon dioxide
- Water and others
- Nitrogen

21%
0.04%
0.96%
78%

78% 2% 4% 16%

Trachea diameter: 0.7 in. (18mm)

Bronchus diameter: 0.5 in. (12mm)

Bronchiole diameter: 0.02 in. (0.6mm)

Alveoli

If they were laid side by side, the alveoli in an adult's lung would cover an area the size of a tennis court.

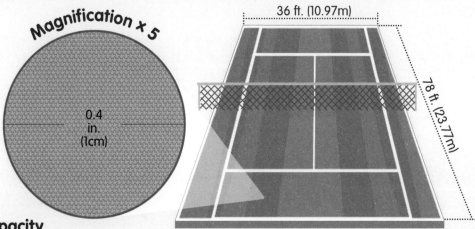

Magnification x 5

0.4 in. (1cm)

36 ft. (10.97m)

78 ft. (23.77m)

Lung capacity

The lungs of adults are about the same size as balls for sports.

Soccerball

Football

Man's lungs
Maximum volume:
1.6 gallons (6L)

Woman's lungs
Maximum volume:
1.1 gallons (4.2L)

Airflow speeds

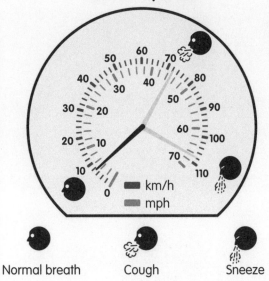

- km/h
- mph

50 60 70 80 90 100 110

Normal breath   Cough   Sneeze

At rest and at play

Your breathing is deeper and slower at rest than during intense physical activity.

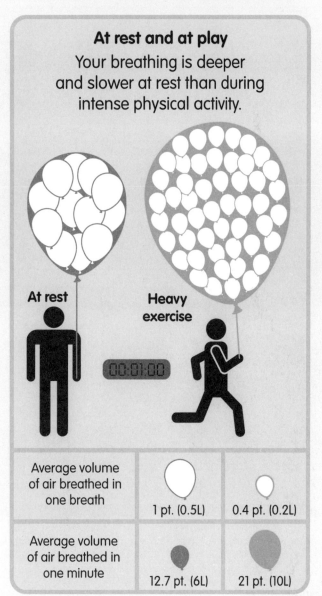

At rest

Heavy exercise

00:01:00

Average volume of air breathed in one breath	1 pt. (0.5L)	0.4 pt. (0.2L)
Average volume of air breathed in one minute	12.7 pt. (6L)	21 pt. (10L)

It's in the blood!

Blood is a transportation system that travels through the veins and arteries in your body, delivering oxygen and essential chemicals to where they are needed. At the same time, blood picks up toxins from around the body and carries them to the organs responsible for getting rid of waste. Blood also helps us fight infections. More than half of our blood is made up of a clear, pale yellow liquid called plasma. Platelets, red blood cells, and white blood cells float in this watery fluid, alongside chemicals such as hormones.

What is in blood?

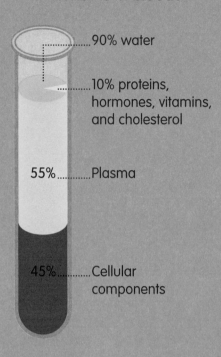

90% water

10% proteins, hormones, vitamins, and cholesterol

55%.............Plasma

45%............Cellular components

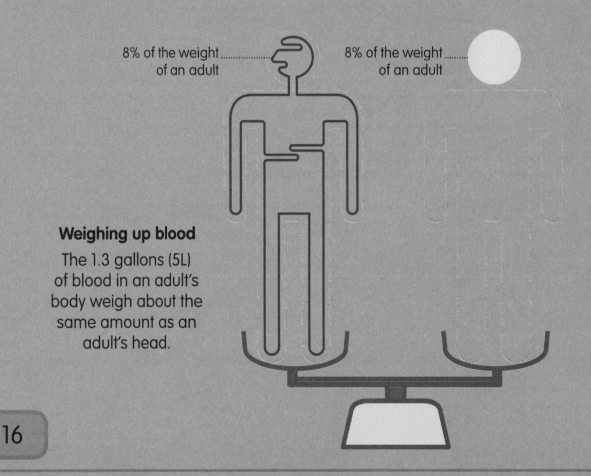

8% of the weight of an adult

8% of the weight of an adult

Weighing up blood

The 1.3 gallons (5L) of blood in an adult's body weigh about the same amount as an adult's head.

Cellular components

There are 600 red blood cells for every one white blood cell and every 40 platelets in blood.

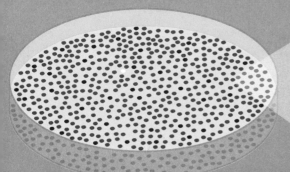

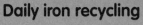 White blood cell

Red blood cell

Platelet

Hemoglobin 33%

Blood-red cell

An iron-rich protein called hemoglobin gives red blood cells their color.

Daily iron recycling

When red blood cells die, they release iron back into the blood system.

25mg

Oxygen transporter

One hemoglobin molecule can carry four oxygen molecules.

Transportation network

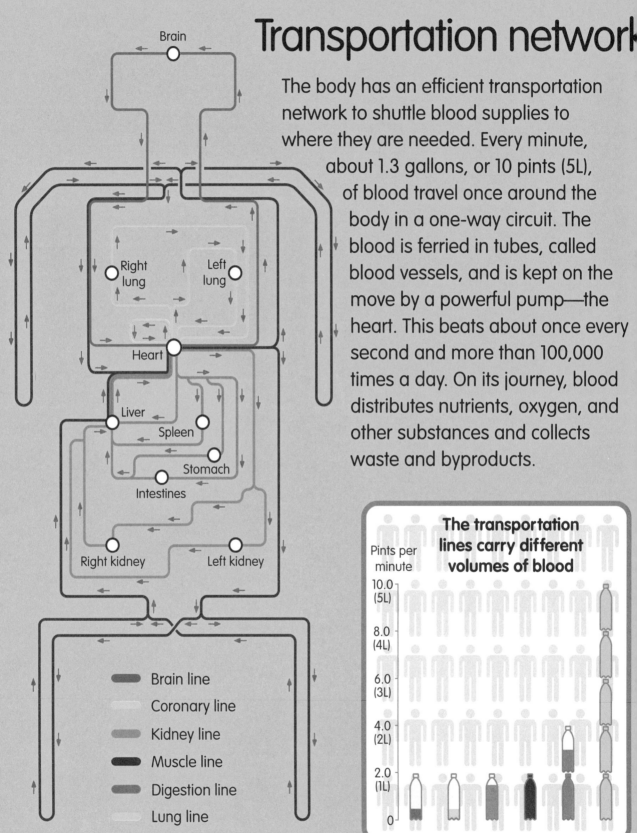

The body has an efficient transportation network to shuttle blood supplies to where they are needed. Every minute, about 1.3 gallons, or 10 pints (5L), of blood travel once around the body in a one-way circuit. The blood is ferried in tubes, called blood vessels, and is kept on the move by a powerful pump—the heart. This beats about once every second and more than 100,000 times a day. On its journey, blood distributes nutrients, oxygen, and other substances and collects waste and byproducts.

Brain

Right lung

Left lung

Heart

Liver

Spleen

Stomach

Intestines

Right kidney

Left kidney

Brain line
Coronary line
Kidney line
Muscle line
Digestion line
Lung line

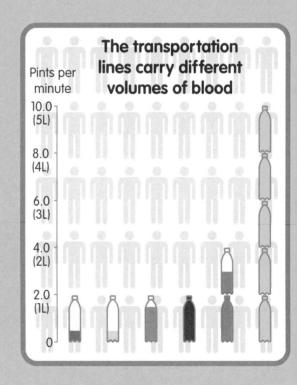

The transportation lines carry different volumes of blood

Pints per minute

10.0 (5L)

8.0 (4L)

6.0 (3L)

4.0 (2L)

2.0 (1L)

0

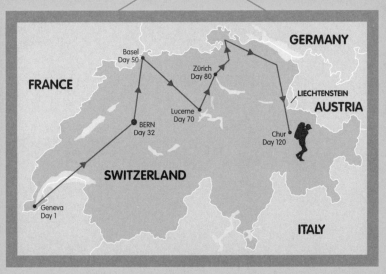

A blood cell travels about 300 miles (480km) in its 120-day lifetime, shown here as a trek across Switzerland.

A beating heart pumps huge volumes of blood as time passes by . . .

• 1 minute: 1.3 gallons/5L (1 small gas can)

• 1 hour: 80 gallons/300L (more than 2 oil barrels)

• 1 day: 1,900 gallons/7,200L (almost 45 oil barrels)

If laid end to end, our blood vessels would stretch 93,200 miles (150,000km), or nearly four times around the world.

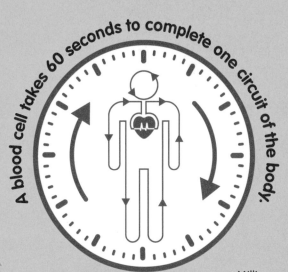

A blood cell takes 60 seconds to complete one circuit of the body.

Million barrels
- 2.0
- 1.5
- 1.0
- 0.5
- 0

• 70 years: 49 million gallons/184 million L (1.2 million oil barrels), filling more than half the capacity of a supertanker

The skin you're in

Without skin, your body's organs and fluid parts would spill out. They would also be exposed to harmful microbes, the weather, and bumps and knocks. You would not experience the sensations of touch and temperature, and your body could overheat or freeze. Human skin has three layers. The outer one, the epidermis, is shed and replaced approximately every 35 days.

The many roles of your hard-working skin

Natural sunscreen
that protects the body from the sun's harmful ultraviolet (UV) rays

Body armor,
made up of fat, that protects the organs and bones by absorbing shock

Sensory organ
that responds to physical contact, heat, cold, vibration, pressure, and pain

Temperature controller
that uses hair, blood vessels, and sweat glands to keep your body at the ideal temperature of 98.6°F (37°C)

Vitamin maker
that uses sunlight to make vitamin D

Infection fighter
that detects microbes and defends your body against them

Waterproof coat
that prevents substances from getting into your body and moisture from getting out

Skin structure

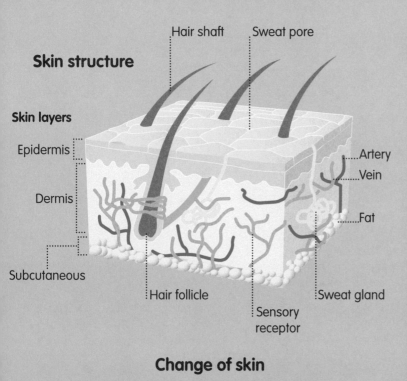

Skin layers

- Epidermis
- Dermis
- Subcutaneous

Hair shaft
Sweat pore
Artery
Vein
Fat
Hair follicle
Sensory receptor
Sweat gland

Sweat soda

11 fl. oz. (330ml)

The sweat glands in an adult's feet can produce enough fluid in one day to fill a soda can.

Change of skin

You shed about 10.4 epidermal skin layers each year.

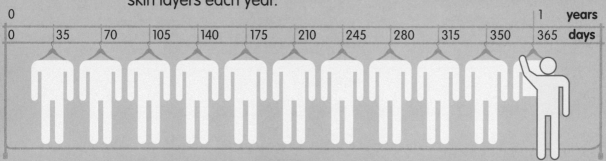

0											1	years
0	35	70	105	140	175	210	245	280	315	350	365	days

How long is your skin safe from sun damage in different levels of UV intensity?

Minutes in the sun without extra protection

0   10   20   30   40   50   60   70   80   90   100   110   120

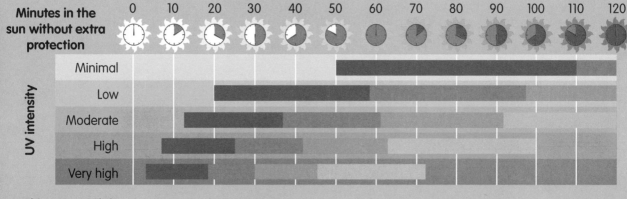

UV intensity
- Minimal
- Low
- Moderate
- High
- Very high

Skin type and the time range in which sun damage first occurs

- ■ Skin that always burns
- ■ Skin that usually burns
- Skin that sometimes burns
- Skin that rarely burns

21

From head to toe

You may think of your hair and nails only as things to be styled and trimmed, but they actually have more practical uses. The millions of hairs all over your body insulate you against the cold, while the hard surface of your nails helps protect the tips of your fingers and toes. Of course, your nails are also useful for scratching an itch! Hair and nails are modified forms of the top layer of your skin—they are all formed from a substance called keratin.

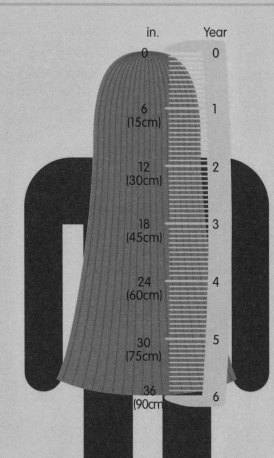

in.	Year
0	0
6 (15cm)	1
12 (30cm)	2
18 (45cm)	3
24 (60cm)	4
30 (75cm)	5
36 (90cm)	6

The long and short of it
Each strand of your head hair can grow up to 6 in. (15cm) every year and has a lifespan of six years.

13 tons (12t)

100,000 strands of hair

Elephant strength
All the hair on your head combined is strong enough to support the weight of two elephants.

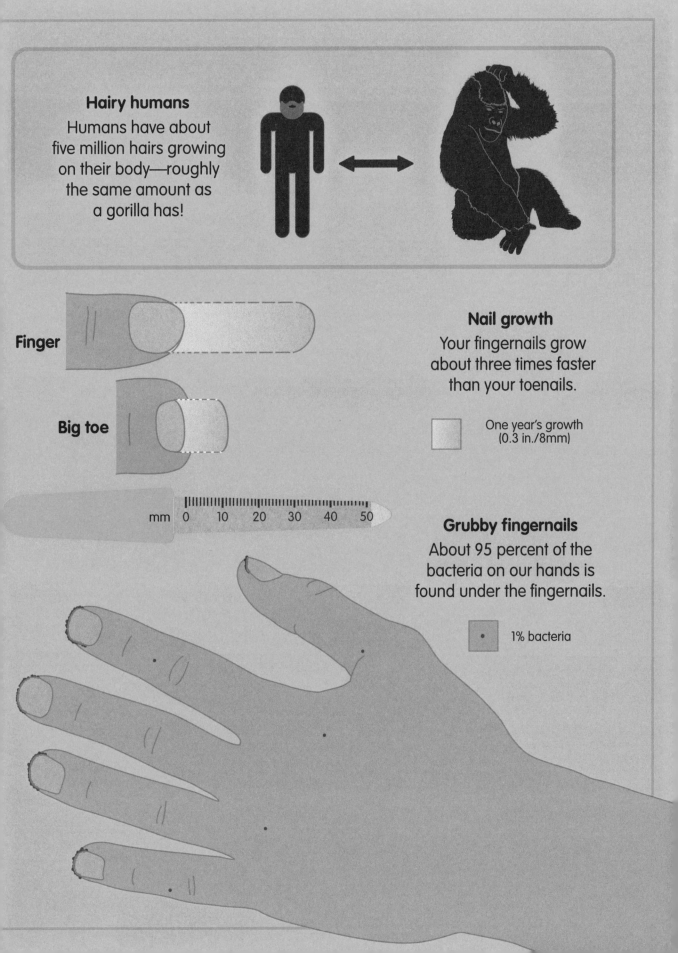

Hairy humans

Humans have about five million hairs growing on their body—roughly the same amount as a gorilla has!

Finger

Big toe

mm 0 10 20 30 40 50

Nail growth

Your fingernails grow about three times faster than your toenails.

One year's growth
(0.3 in./8mm)

Grubby fingernails

About 95 percent of the bacteria on our hands is found under the fingernails.

• 1% bacteria

Body defenses

The body is designed to protect itself against infectious microbes. Your skin forms an external defensive layer. If you cut yourself, your blood forms a scab that stops microbes from getting in. Most of the microbes that get into your mouth drop into your stomach acid and are killed. Hairs in your nose filter the air you breathe in. If nasty microbes get past these defenses, an army of white blood cells swallows up and destroys the invaders.

A timeline for wound healing

Days 0 to 2
Blood clots and scab begins to form

Day 3
Cells multiply to make new skin tissue

Weeks to months
Skin reforms, closing the wound

Lines of defense

First line of defense
Physical barriers

Second line of defense
Producers and developers of white blood cells

Concentrations of white blood cells

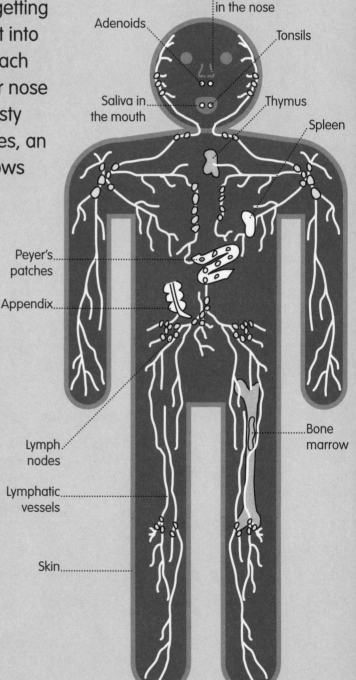

Hair and mucus in the nose

Adenoids

Tonsils

Saliva in the mouth

Thymus

Spleen

Peyer's patches

Appendix

Lymph nodes

Lymphatic vessels

Bone marrow

Skin

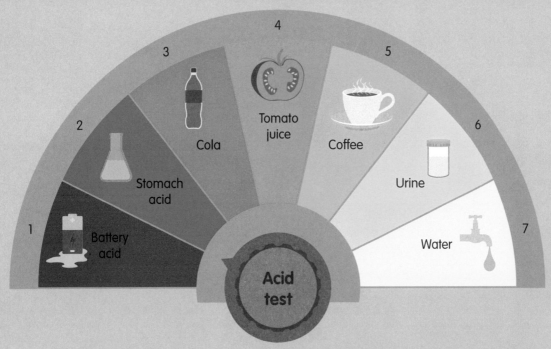

This scale shows how acidic or alkaline certain fluids are. Battery acid is the most acidic of the fluids shown. Stomach acid is also a strong acid, so it would have no trouble killing infectious microbes.

White blood cells at war

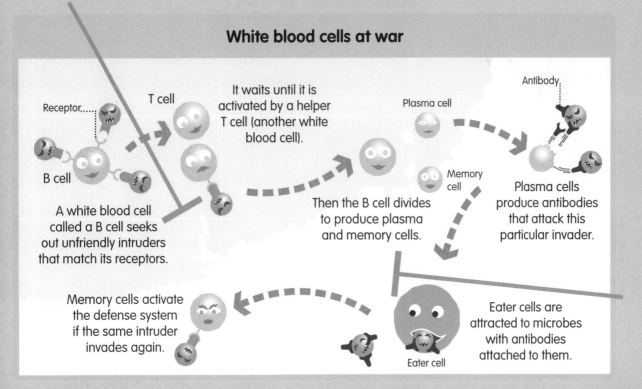

A white blood cell called a B cell seeks out unfriendly intruders that match its receptors.

It waits until it is activated by a helper T cell (another white blood cell).

Then the B cell divides to produce plasma and memory cells.

Plasma cells produce antibodies that attack this particular invader.

Eater cells are attracted to microbes with antibodies attached to them.

Memory cells activate the defense system if the same intruder invades again.

0 minutes	20 minutes	40 minutes	60 minutes

Alien invasion
Bacteria splits in two every 20 minutes. If invading
bacteria were left to develop, there could be enough
to cover the entire surface of Earth within 36 hours.

Body invaders

When unfriendly microbes, such as bacteria and viruses,
invade your body, they reproduce very rapidly, damaging your
body tissues as they multiply. Your body responds to this damage
with symptoms, such as coughing, fevers, aches, and tiredness. It
is these symptoms that make you feel sick. Viruses and bacterial
infections can be spread through the air or through contact with
things that have the harmful microbes on them.

Cell invaders
Three steps to a
successful viral invasion

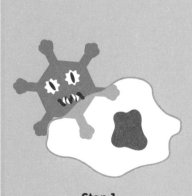  

Step 1
A single virus
takes over a cell.

Step 2
The virus uses the cell to
make duplicate viruses.

Step 3
Viruses burst out, destroying
the cell on the way, ready to
infect more cells.

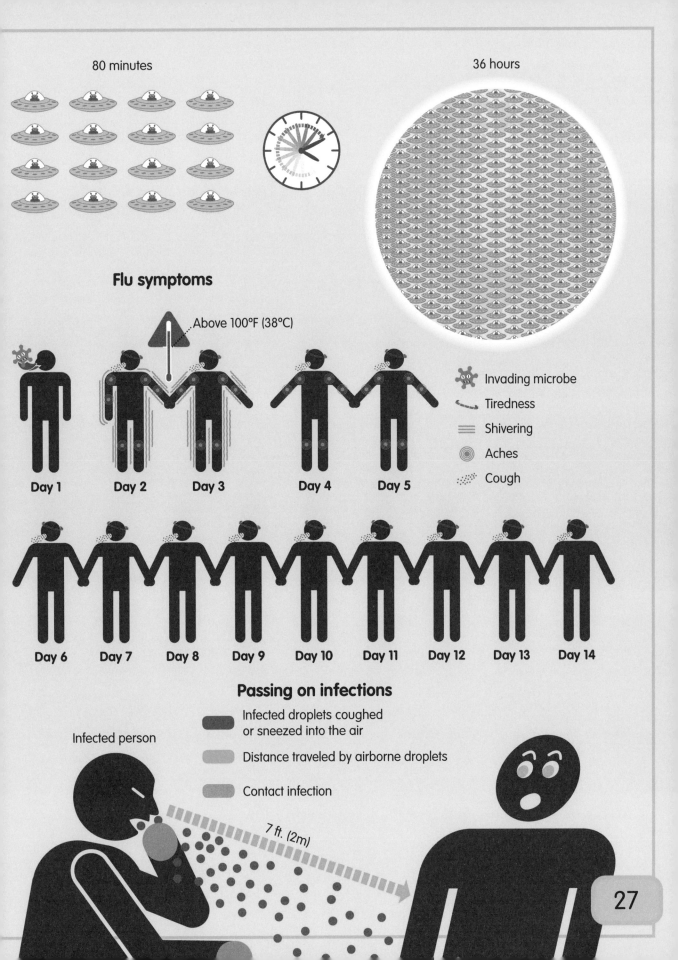

80 minutes

36 hours

Flu symptoms

Above 100°F (38°C)

Day 1
Day 2
Day 3
Day 4
Day 5

Invading microbe
Tiredness
Shivering
Aches
Cough

Day 6
Day 7
Day 8
Day 9
Day 10
Day 11
Day 12
Day 13
Day 14

Passing on infections

Infected droplets coughed or sneezed into the air

Distance traveled by airborne droplets

Contact infection

Infected person

7 ft. (2m)

Water of life

More than half of your weight is made up of water. Your body needs this water to carry out essential processes. For example, water removes wastes from your vital organs, carries nutrients to your cells, and regulates your body temperature. You lose water from your body when you urinate, sweat, and breathe out. If you don't replace this water by drinking and eating, you become dehydrated.

Water in the body
The amount of water in your body reduces as you get older.

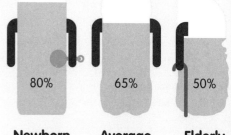

Newborn baby	Average adult	Elderly person
80%	65%	50%

Water in the average adult's organs, bones, and teeth

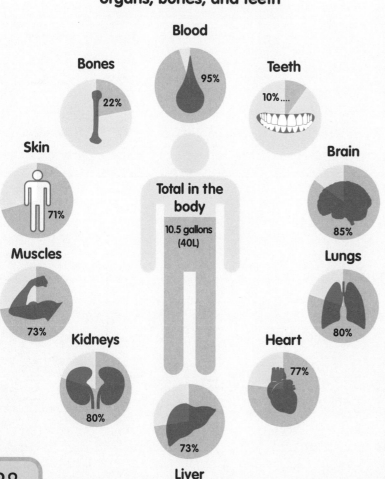

Bones 22%

Blood 95%

Teeth 10%....

Skin 71%

Total in the body 10.5 gallons (40L)

Brain 85%

Muscles 73%

Lungs 80%

Kidneys 80%

Heart 77%

Liver 73%

Water in food

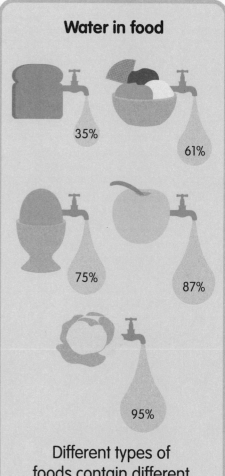

35%

61%

75%

87%

95%

Different types of foods contain different percentages of water.

Water levels

Our body must maintain a balance between the water we take in and the water we lose.

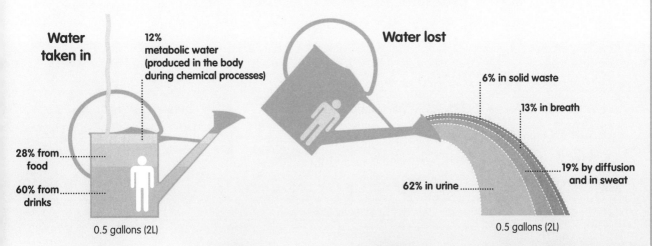

Water taken in

12% metabolic water (produced in the body during chemical processes)

28% from food

60% from drinks

0.5 gallons (2L)

Water lost

6% in solid waste

13% in breath

19% by diffusion and in sweat

62% in urine

0.5 gallons (2L)

Stages of dehydration

The symptoms of dehydration become more serious the more water you lose.

Symptoms

0.4 gallons (1L)

0.8 gallons (3L)

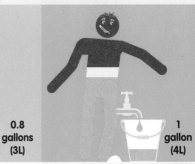

1 gallon (4L)

| Thirst | Sluggishness, extreme tiredness, nausea, and emotional instability | Clumsiness, headaches, plus increased body temperature, pulse rate, and breathing rate |

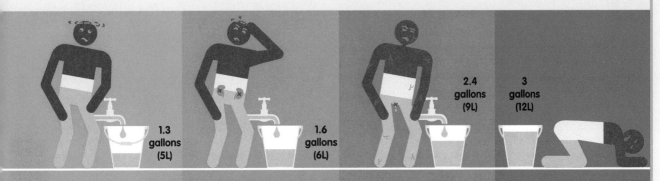

1.3 gallons (5L)

1.6 gallons (6L)

2.4 gallons (9L)

3 gallons (12L)

| Dizziness, slurred speech, weakness, and confusion | Delirium, swollen tongue, circulatory problems, decreased blood volume, and kidney failure | Inability to swallow, painful urination, and cracked skin | Life-threatening level of dehydration |

29

Waste disposal

Your body creates a variety of wastes while it carries out essential chemical processes. Most of these wastes are filtered from your blood by two organs called kidneys. The kidneys return useful substances to the body system. They also send excess water and waste in the form of urine (pee) down tubes to a baglike organ known as the bladder. When this is full, your brain tells you to release the urine by going to the bathroom.

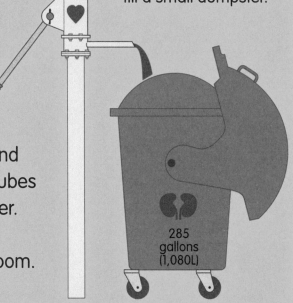

The volume of blood that the heart pumps to the kidneys each day would fill a small dumpster.

285 gallons (1,080L)

Urine sample

A healthy person's urine contains these substances (right), roughly in the amounts shown.

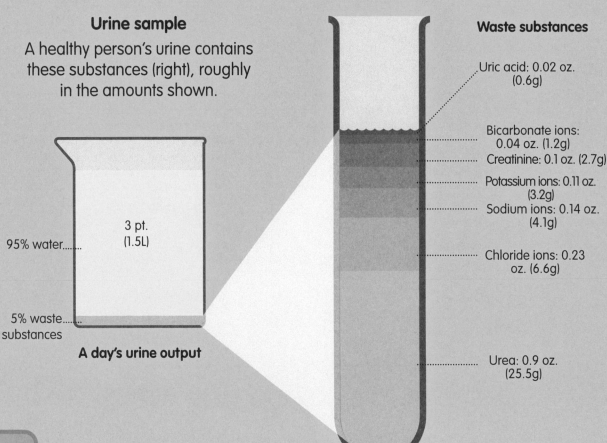

3 pt. (1.5L)

95% water......

5% waste...... substances

A day's urine output

Waste substances

Uric acid: 0.02 oz. (0.6g)

Bicarbonate ions: 0.04 oz. (1.2g)

Creatinine: 0.1 oz. (2.7g)

Potassium ions: 0.11 oz. (3.2g)

Sodium ions: 0.14 oz. (4.1g)

Chloride ions: 0.23 oz. (6.6g)

Urea: 0.9 oz. (25.5g)

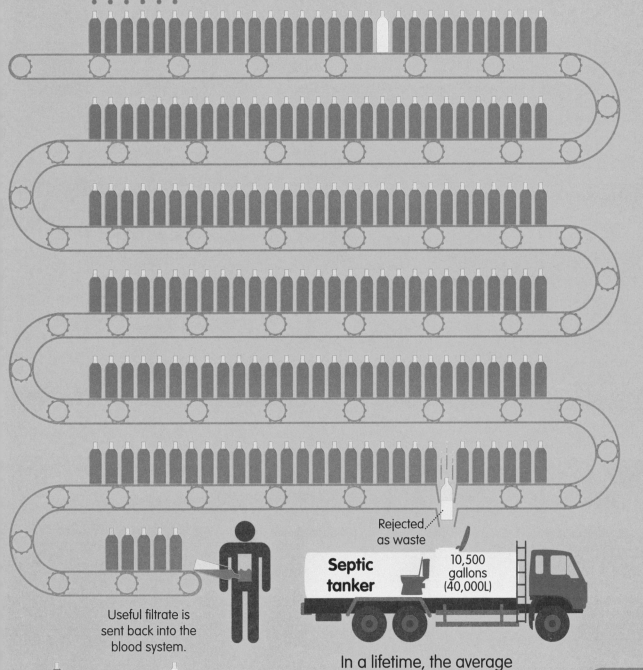

Blood pumped from the heart

Blood sent back into the blood system

Blood filtration system

Filtrate, made up of water and dissolved substances

Filtration and disposal

The filtration system removes 48 gallons (180L) of fluid from the blood. Of this amount, 3 pints, or 0.4 gallons (1.5L), are urine, which is expelled as waste.

Rejected as waste

Septic tanker

10,500 gallons (40,000L)

Useful filtrate is sent back into the blood system.

2 pt. (1L) of filtrate

2 pt. (1L) of urine

In a lifetime, the average human produces enough urine to fill a septic tanker.

31

Coping with extremes

Our bodies have heat-regulation systems that help us stay at an optimum (ideal) temperature of 98.6°F (37°C) in warm and cold conditions. But our bodies can't cope with extremes of cold and heat or low oxygen levels. We have learned to overcome these conditions by adopting survival strategies, such as wearing warm clothing, running air conditioning, and using an air supply.

98.6°F
(37°C)

77°F
(25°C)

Temperature control

When it gets cold, the body diverts heat to the core organs.

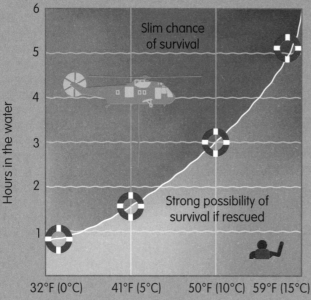

Cold water survival time

Slim chance of survival

Strong possibility of survival if rescued

6

5

4

3

2

1

Hours in the water

32°F (0°C)   41°F (5°C)   50°F (10°C)   59°F (15°C)

Water temperature

Headaches and dizziness

No symptoms

Hazards of a decreasing core temperature

The stages of hypothermia

98.6–95°F (37–35°C) Shivering

Legend

☾ Percentage of oxygen available

▨ Height above sea level

These pictures show the symptoms suffered by a person who is unused to high altitudes, and who is climbing without an air supply.

Death is likely

Mount Everest 29,029 ft. (8,848m)

29,528 ft. (9,000m)
33%

Organs begin to shut down

26,247 ft. (8,000m)
37%

Hallucinations

24,606 ft. (7,500m)
40%

Can't remember what you are supposed to be doing

Aconcagua 22,841 ft. (6,962m)

19,685 ft. (6,000m)
49%

Inability to figure out what is around you

Kilimanjaro 19,341 ft. (5,895m)

16,404 ft. (5,000m)
55%

Mont Blanc 15,774 ft. (4,808m)

Inability to control the movement of the hands

11,483 ft. (3,500m)
66%

8,202 ft. (2,500m)
75%

Ben Nevis 4,409 ft. (1,344m)

3,281 ft. (1,000m)
89%

93–91°F (34–33°C) Nausea and disorientation

89.6–82.4°F (32–28°C) Unconsciousness

33

Mind control

The brain is the body's control center. It operates all necessary functions of the body, such as regulating your heartbeat and breathing, sending you to sleep, and telling your body how to move. But the brain also receives and interprets information from the outside world, allows you to think, stores your memories, gives you personality, and controls your emotions. The brain governs all these things by sending and receiving millions of tiny electrical signals through a network of billions of nerve cells, called neurons.

Brain power
The brain uses 23 watts of energy, which is enough to power a light bulb.

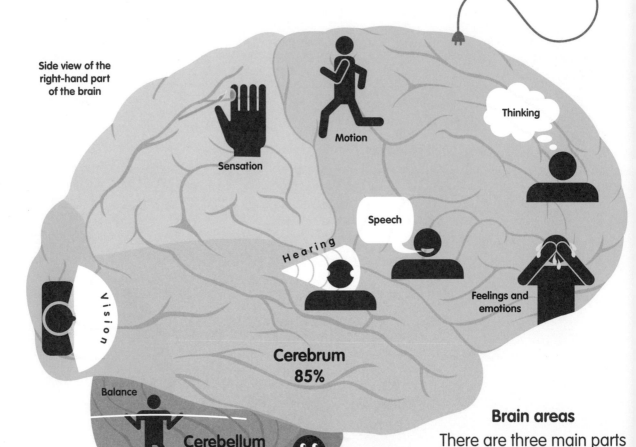

Side view of the right-hand part of the brain

Sensation

Motion

Thinking

Speech

Hearing

Vision

Feelings and emotions

Cerebrum
85%

Balance

Cerebellum
11%

Eye and face movement

Brain areas
There are three main parts of the brain. Areas within these parts are responsible for different functions.

Breathing and heart rate

Brain stem
4%

Thoughtful brain
You think 70,000 thoughts a day.

Oxygen use
Your brain uses about 20 percent of the oxygen you inhale (take in).

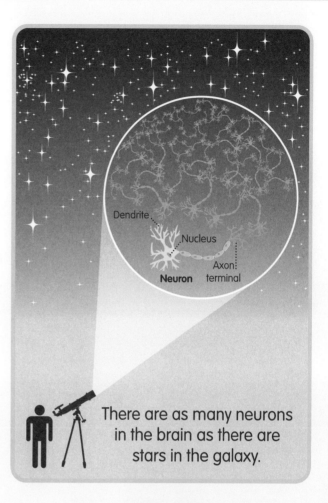

Dendrite

Nucleus

Axon terminal

Neuron

There are as many neurons in the brain as there are stars in the galaxy.

A brain of two halves
The left half of the brain is the logical side. The right half is the creative side.

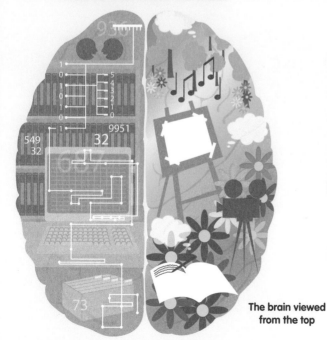

The brain viewed from the top

Brain size
The average brain is the size of a cantaloupe (a small melon) and weighs about 3 pounds (1.4kg).

The body's Internet

Your body has built-in wiring and communications in the form of the nervous system. This coordinates and controls almost all your body's activities. It works much like the system that we use to make telephone calls and surf the Internet. Both are designed to send messages from one place to another. The messages travel in the form of electrical signals or pulses, along bundles of wirelike structures. The body's wires are called nerves.

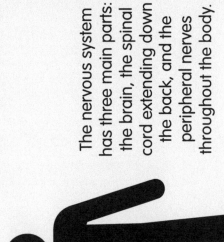

The nervous system has three main parts: the brain, the spinal cord extending down the back, and the peripheral nerves throughout the body.

Peripheral nervous system
A network of nerves that branch out from the brain and spinal cord to every part of the body.

Central nervous system
This consists of the brain and spinal cord, which links the brain to many parts of the body.

Autonomic nervous system

This deals with automatic body processes. These happen on their own without our awareness.

Parasympathetic   **Sympathetic**

Constricts pupils — Dilates pupils

Slows down heartbeat — Accelerates heartbeat

Dilates bronchi — Constricts bronchi

Contracts bladder — Inhibits bladder contraction

Somatic nervous system

Some of the messages are about sensations, and others are about movements that we make at will and control with our thoughts.

Touch

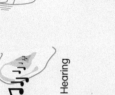
Hearing

Eye movement

Releasing urine from the bladder

Limb movement

Message speeds

Message to

Muscle

Message from Brain

390 ft. (119m) per second

Touch

250 ft. (76.2m) per second

Brain

Pain

2 ft. (0.61m) per second

Brain

Distance traveled in 1 second

Reflex action

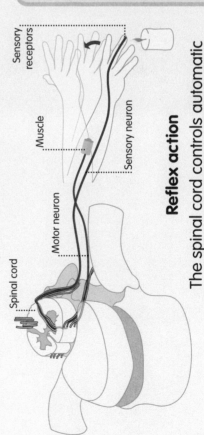

Spinal cord

Motor neuron

Muscle

Sensory receptors

Sensory neuron

The spinal cord controls automatic and rapid actions called reflexes. These include snatching your hand away from the heat of a flame.

37

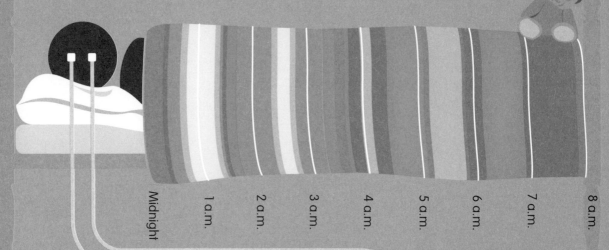

A good night's sleep
Four stages of deep NREM sleep are
followed by lighter REM sleep, during which
the eyes move back and forth rapidly.

Midnight | 1 a.m. | 2 a.m. | 3 a.m. | 4 a.m. | 5 a.m. | 6 a.m. | 7 a.m. | 8 a.m.

Sleepyheads

It may seem like we do nothing when we sleep; however, the brain is actually very active during this time. Scientists use an EEG machine to detect and display brain waves—the patterns of electrical activity produced by the brain cells. The EEG pattern changes in a predictable way several times during a single period of sleep. There are two basic forms of sleep: rapid eye movement (REM) sleep and nonrapid REM (NREM) sleep.

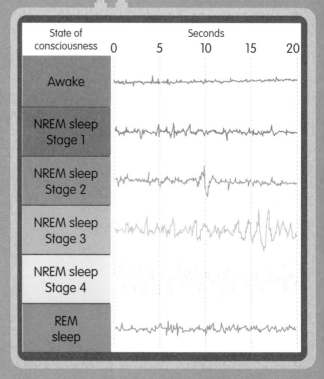

Brain wave activity
There are fewer brain waves during
NREM sleep than REM sleep.

Sweet dreams

An adult has about five dreams in one night, usually during REM sleep.

Hours of sleep in a 24-hour period

Age of sleeping person

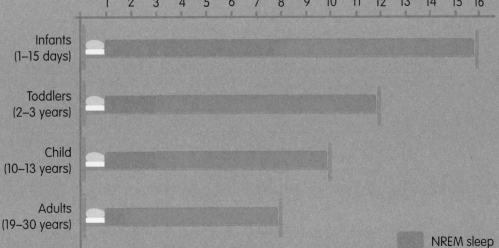

Infants
(1–15 days)

Toddlers
(2–3 years)

Child
(10–13 years)

Adults
(19–30 years)

Elderly person
(70–85 years)

NREM sleep

REM sleep

Work, rest, and play

On average, people spend about one third of the year asleep.

33%
.................122 days

67%
243 days.................

Sight

Your eyes take pictures of the world around you, then send them to your brain for processing. A lens in your eye acts like a camera lens, focusing light rays onto the inside lining of the back wall of the eye, called the retina. Here, special cells record the pattern created by the rays and send the information to the brain. The brain then figures out what your eyes are seeing.

Cross section of a human eye

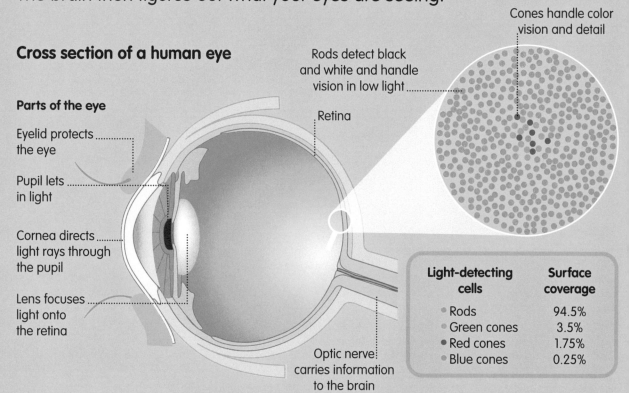

Cones handle color vision and detail

Rods detect black and white and handle vision in low light

Retina

Parts of the eye

Eyelid protects the eye

Pupil lets in light

Cornea directs light rays through the pupil

Lens focuses light onto the retina

Optic nerve carries information to the brain

Light-detecting cells	Surface coverage
Rods	94.5%
Green cones	3.5%
Red cones	1.75%
Blue cones	0.25%

Hearing

As with your sight, your hearing gives your brain information about what is happening around you. The sounds that you hear, such as people talking, are created by invisible vibrations called sound waves. These travel through the air in all directions. Your ears collect the sound waves and first turn them into mechanical vibrations, then electrical signals that your brain can understand.

Light, lens, action

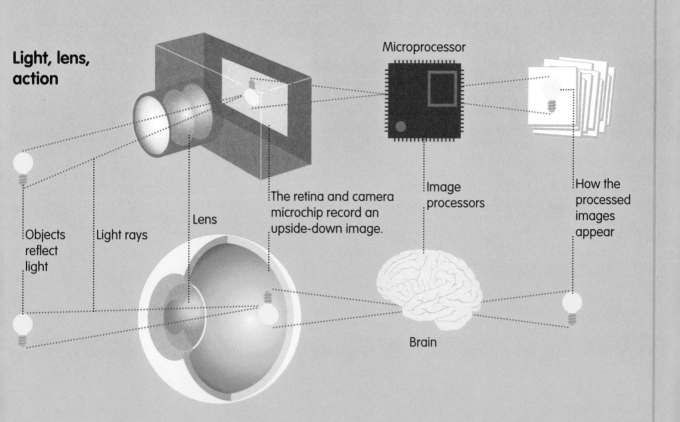

Microprocessor

Objects reflect light

Light rays

Lens

The retina and camera microchip record an upside-down image.

Image processors

How the processed images appear

Brain

Hear and how

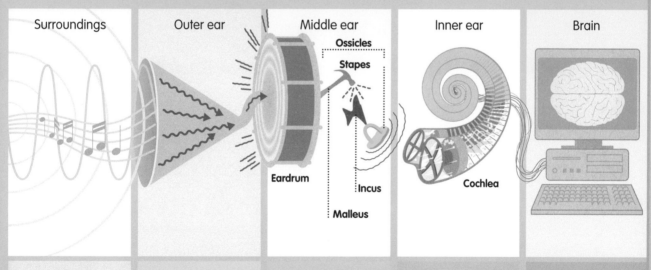

Surroundings	Outer ear	Middle ear	Inner ear	Brain
		Ossicles, Stapes, Eardrum, Incus, Malleus	Cochlea	
Reception Invisible sound waves move through the air and approach your ears.	**Collection** Your trumpet-shaped outer ear collects sound waves and directs them toward your eardrum.	**Vibration** The waves strike the eardrum, causing it and the tiny ossicle bones to vibrate and create pressure waves.	**Electrical notes** Fluid in the inner ear is forced over structures that, similar to keyboard keys, convert the pressure into electrical signals.	**Processing** Electrical signals are sent to the brain, where they are processed so that you hear sound.

Smell and taste

Our senses of smell and taste work in similar ways. Groups of olfactory cells in the nose detect floating molecules of scent in the air, called odorants. The nose can distinguish more than 10,000 different scents. Taste buds in the mouth detect flavorants, but our mouths pick up only five basic flavors. As we eat, the brain receives information from both senses. It comes to associate the odors with the flavors, creating an overall "taste sensation."

▲ 20% intensity ▲ 100% intensity

Familiar scent
The odor of perfume is only one fifth as powerful to a person who usually wears it than it is to other people.

Reception area
The 12 million olfactory receptor cells in your nose cover an area about the size of a rose petal.

Olfactory receptor cells

Odorant molecule

1.5 square in.
(10 square cm)

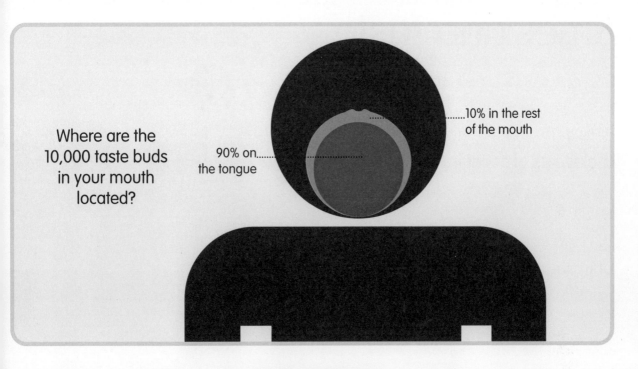

Where are the 10,000 taste buds in your mouth located?

90% on the tongue

........10% in the rest of the mouth

Five basic flavors

Our taste buds register differing proportions of these flavors in different foods and drinks.

Sweet

Sour

Salty

Bitter

Umami

Taste sensation
Without our sense of smell, our food would be about 80 percent less flavorsome.

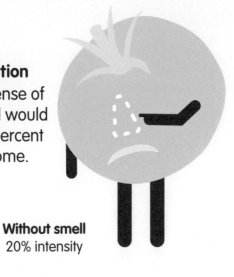

Without smell
20% intensity

With smell
100% intensity

43

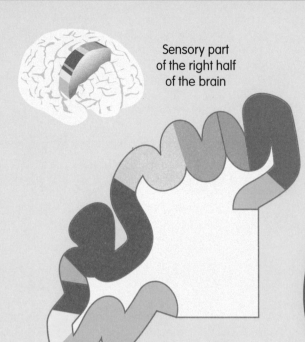

Sensory part of the right half of the brain

Sensory body map

The most sensitive areas of the body have the highest density of sensors, which are connected to the largest sensory processing areas in the brain.

Above: here are the relative amounts of brain area that process sensory information from the parts of the body shown in the same colors on the right.

Right: this shows what a human body would look like if each part grew in proportion to the area of the brain concerned with its sensory perception. The larger areas in this picture are the most sensitive.

Touch

Millions of sensors in your skin allow you to feel a range of sensations, from the pain of touching a hot flame to the tickling of a feather as it brushes against your skin. The receptors send messages along nerves to the spinal cord and the sensory part of the brain, where the information is processed.

Hot spots

Your head and hands have the greatest concentration of heat sensors in your body.

Thick and thin skin

Sensors in the thin skin on your forehead can detect the weight of a 2-milligram fruit fly, but you wouldn't sense it on the thick skin of your fingertip.

Sensory thermometer

Here are the temperatures at which you detect the sensations of heat, cold, pain, and numbness.

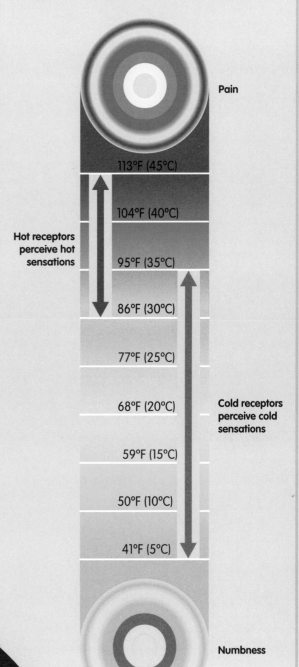

Pain

113°F (45°C)

104°F (40°C)

Hot receptors perceive hot sensations

95°F (35°C)

86°F (30°C)

77°F (25°C)

68°F (20°C)

Cold receptors perceive cold sensations

59°F (15°C)

50°F (10°C)

41°F (5°C)

Numbness

Moving around

The human body is a mechanical masterpiece capable of performing a huge range of movements. Without its framework of bones, called the skeleton, and the skeletal muscles that cover it, your body would be a motionless blob on the ground. Joints between the bones make your skeleton flexible. Under the control of your brain, your muscles contract or relax to move your bones at the joints, allowing you to run, jump, and perform many other movements.

Where bones meet

The type of joint that connects two bones determines how those bones move in relation to each other.

Pivot joints (neck and forearm) allow one bone to rotate around another.

Ball and socket joints (shoulders and hips) permit movement in almost every direction.

Hinge joints (elbow and knee) enable movement much like the opening and closing of a hinged door.

Saddle joints (thumbs) allow movement back and forth and from side to side.

Plane joints (wrists and ankles) allow sliding or gliding movements.

Ellipsoid joints (fingers) allow movement back and forth, side to side, plus a very small amount of rotation.

Your main muscle groups

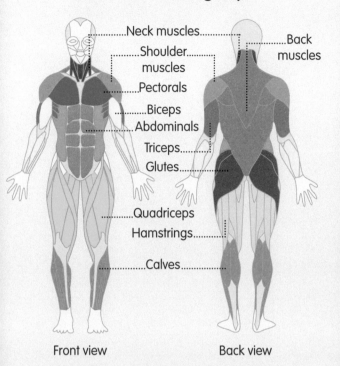

Neck muscles
Shoulder muscles
Pectorals
Biceps
Abdominals
Triceps
Glutes
Quadriceps
Hamstrings
Calves

Back muscles

Front view   Back view

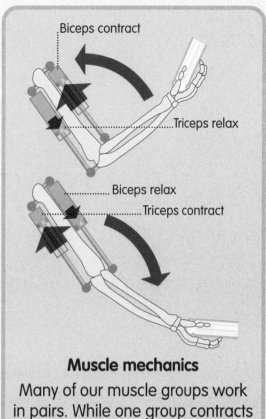

Biceps contract
Triceps relax

Biceps relax
Triceps contract

Muscle mechanics

Many of our muscle groups work in pairs. While one group contracts (shortens), the other group relaxes. This makes the bones move.

Pedal power

Here are the leg muscles you use when you pedal your bike.

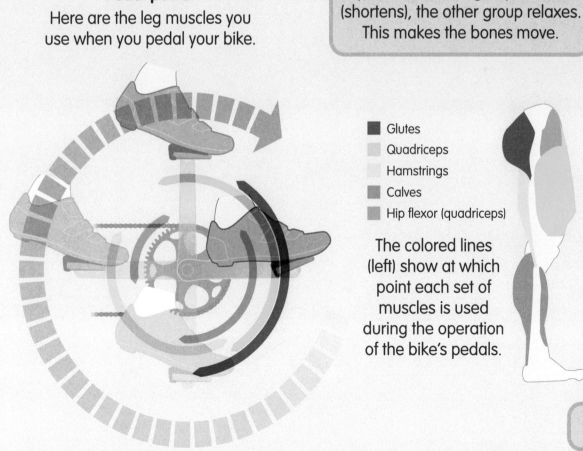

- Glutes
- Quadriceps
- Hamstrings
- Calves
- Hip flexor (quadriceps)

The colored lines (left) show at which point each set of muscles is used during the operation of the bike's pedals.

New life

There are around seven billion people in the world, and they all began in the same way. The male reproductive system makes cells, called sperm, that fertilize, or fuse with, a female egg cell to make a fertilized egg. This forms an embryo that divides repeatedly, producing a fetus after about eight weeks. This grows inside the mother's uterus and develops into a baby.

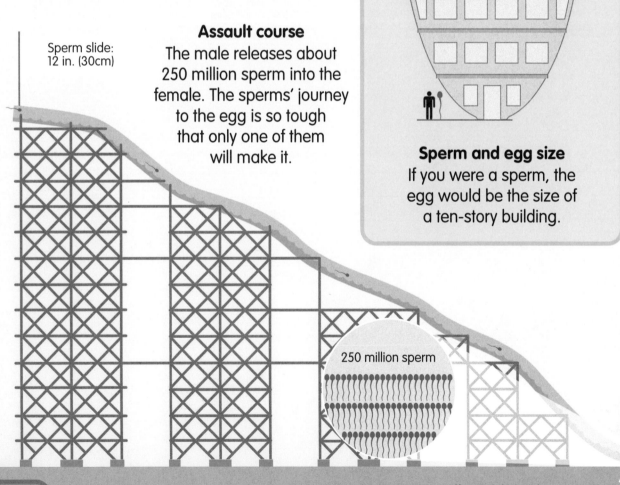

Sperm and egg size
If you were a sperm, the egg would be the size of a ten-story building.

Assault course
The male releases about 250 million sperm into the female. The sperms' journey to the egg is so tough that only one of them will make it.

Sperm slide: 12 in. (30cm)

250 million sperm

Deadly acid pool
The sperm have to endure a 4-in.- (10-cm-) .....
long swim through acidic fluids in the vagina.

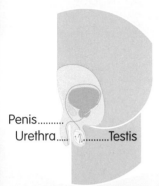

Penis..........
Urethra.......................Testis

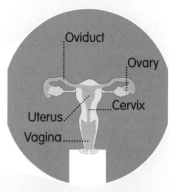

Oviduct
Ovary
Cervix
Uterus..
Vagina..........

Male reproductive system

Sperm are produced in the two testes. They are released through the urethra, which is a tube inside the penis.

Female reproductive system

Each month, one of the ovaries produces a ripe egg cell. This makes its way along the oviduct, toward the uterus.

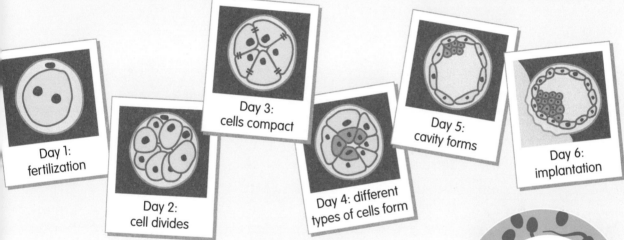

Day 1: fertilization

Day 2: cell divides

Day 3: cells compact

Day 4: different types of cells form

Day 5: cavity forms

Day 6: implantation

Embryo growth

After fertilization, the egg cell splits into several cells and eventually implants itself into the wall of the uterus.

About 60,000 sperm survive the 0.8-in.- (2-cm-) high climb to reach the cervix.

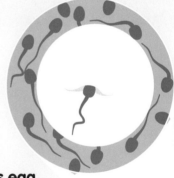

Sperm meets egg

One out of 15 to 24 sperm cells fertilizes the egg.

..........10% survive

90% die

Mazelike cervix

Only 3,000 sperm make it out of the cervix alive.

The gauntlet

About 50 sperm survive the attacks of white blood cells in the uterus.

Lazy river

The 4-in.- (10-cm-) long oviducts are paradise for the sperm.

Growing and developing

It takes more than 20 years for the human body to grow and develop fully. During this time, you lose a set of teeth and replace it with another set. Your body proportions change and you become stronger, so you can do more and more physical things. Your brain also develops, gradually turning you into an independent person capable of making your own decisions—an adult!

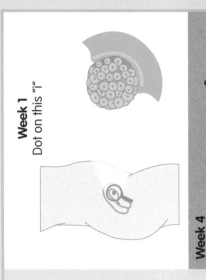
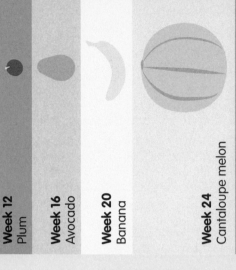

Week 1
Dot on this "i"

Week 4
Poppy seed

Week 8
Raspberry

Week 12
Plum

Week 16
Avocado

Week 20
Banana

Week 24
Cantaloupe melon

Week 28
Eggplant

Becoming mature

One of the last parts of the brain to mature is the area that controls your ability to make sensible decisions and plan out things.

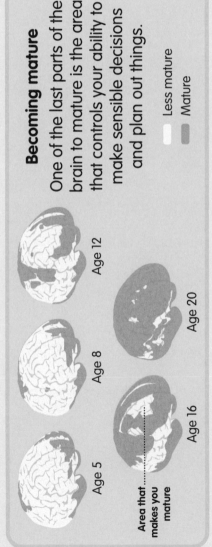

Less mature
Mature

Age 5
Age 8
Age 12
Age 16
Age 20

Area that makes you mature

Teething times
Your baby teeth and permanent teeth appear in the order shown here.

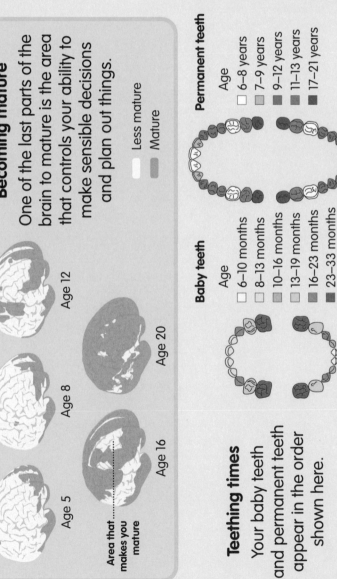

Baby teeth

Age
- 6–10 months
- 8–13 months
- 10–16 months
- 13–19 months
- 16–23 months
- 23–33 months

Permanent teeth

Age
- 6–8 years
- 7–9 years
- 9–12 years
- 11–13 years
- 17–21 years

Week 32
Ambercup squash

Week 36
Honeydew melon

Week 40
Watermelon

Fruit of the womb

During the nine months that it is in the womb (uterus), a baby grows from being the size of the dot on this "i" to the size of a watermelon.

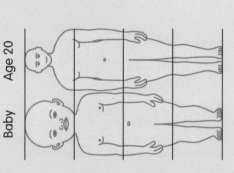

Baby   Age 20

Body proportions

The proportions of the head and arms are very different in babies and adults.

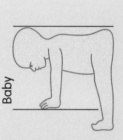

Baby

Age 20

Standing tall

From about five years old, growth gradually slows down. Then from about 10 to 13 years in girls, and 13 to 15 years in boys, growth speeds up again.

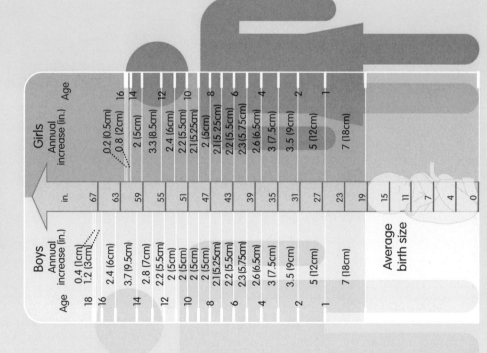

Boys Annual increase (in.)	Age	in.	Age	Girls Annual increase (in.)
0.4 (1cm)	18	67	16	0.2 (0.5cm)
1.2 (3cm)			14	0.8 (2cm)
2.4 (6cm)	16	63		2 (5cm)
3.7 (9.5cm)	14	59	12	3.3 (8.5cm)
2.8 (7cm)		55		2.4 (6cm)
2.2 (5.5cm)	12	51	10	2.2 (5.5cm)
2 (5cm)				2.1 (5.25cm)
2 (5cm)	10	47	8	2 (5cm)
2.1 (5.25cm)	8	43	6	2.1 (5.25cm)
2.2 (5.5cm)				2.2 (5.5cm)
2.3 (5.75cm)	6	39	4	2.3 (5.75cm)
2.6 (6.5cm)		35		2.6 (6.5cm)
3 (7.5cm)	4	31	2	3 (7.5cm)
3.5 (9cm)		27		3.5 (9cm)
5 (12cm)	2	23	1	5 (12cm)
7 (18cm)	1	19		7 (18cm)
	Average birth size	15		
		11		
		7		
		4		
		0		

Code for life

Every cell in your body contains a set of coded instructions that tells the cell what it should be doing and how to do it. The instructions are written in an alphabet that is only four letters long—A, T, C, and G—and they come in the form of a molecule called deoxyribonucleic acid (DNA). This has a twisted ladder shape, known as a double helix. The letters of the DNA alphabet are substances called bases. These make up the "ladder rungs." Sugars and other atoms form the "handrail."

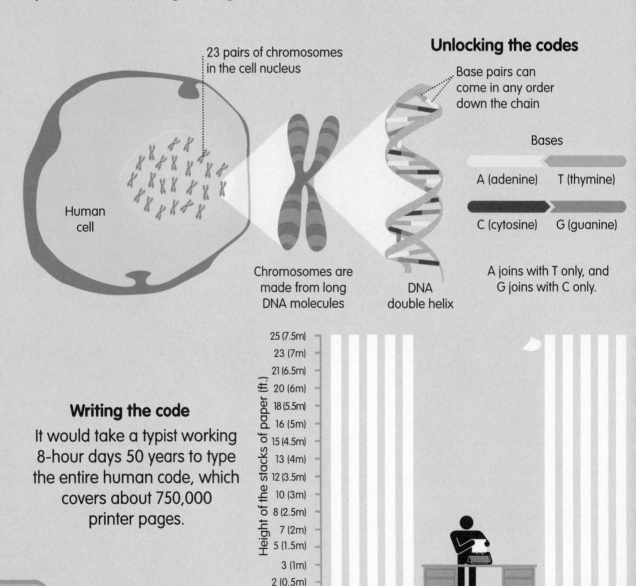

23 pairs of chromosomes in the cell nucleus

Human cell

Chromosomes are made from long DNA molecules

DNA double helix

Unlocking the codes

Base pairs can come in any order down the chain

Bases

A (adenine)   T (thymine)

C (cytosine)   G (guanine)

A joins with T only, and G joins with C only.

Writing the code

It would take a typist working 8-hour days 50 years to type the entire human code, which covers about 750,000 printer pages.

Height of the stacks of paper (ft.)

25 (7.5m)
23 (7m)
21 (6.5m)
20 (6m)
18 (5.5m)
16 (5m)
15 (4.5m)
13 (4m)
12 (3.5m)
10 (3m)
8 (2.5m)
7 (2m)
5 (1.5m)
3 (1m)
2 (0.5m)
0

5   10   15   20   25   Years   30   35   40   45   50

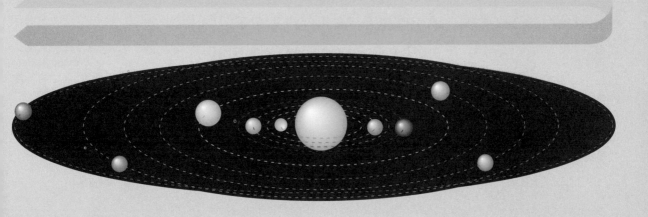

How long is your DNA?

If it were laid end to end, all the DNA in your body would span the diameter of the solar system twice.

Sharing DNA

■ 99% shared DNA   ■ 1% different DNA

Many scientists believe most of our DNA is the same as that of a chimpanzee.

Cracking the code

The purpose of about 95 percent of our DNA has yet to be figured out by scientists.

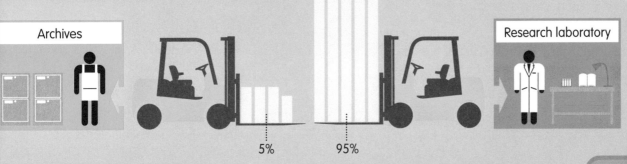

Archives

5%

95%

Research laboratory

It's in the genes!

Segments of DNA called genes determine which physical features we inherit from our parents. Genes carry the codes for making proteins in the cell. Proteins build everything in your body: bones, teeth, hair, muscles, and more. Each parent passes on a copy of their genes to their children. Certain inherited traits dominate over others. For example, if one parent has freckles yet the other parent doesn't, their offspring will have freckles, as this is a dominant trait.

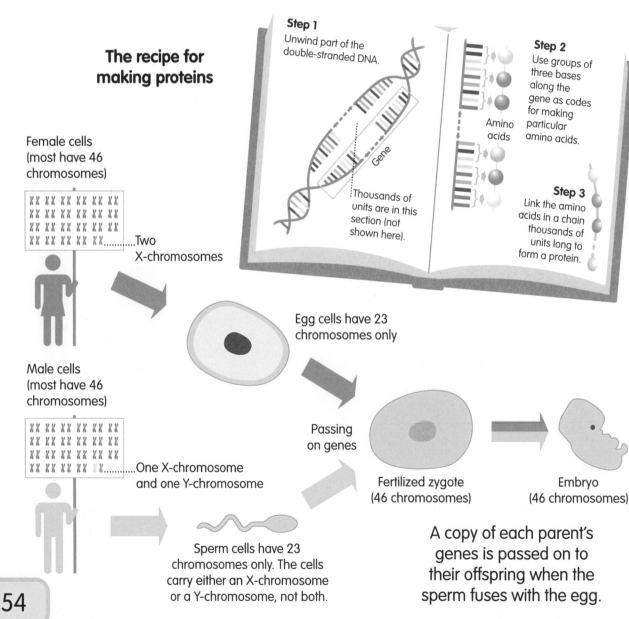

The recipe for making proteins

Step 1
Unwind part of the double-stranded DNA.

Gene

Thousands of units are in this section (not shown here).

Step 2
Use groups of three bases along the gene as codes for making particular amino acids.

Amino acids

Step 3
Link the amino acids in a chain thousands of units long to form a protein.

Female cells (most have 46 chromosomes)

Two X-chromosomes

Male cells (most have 46 chromosomes)

One X-chromosome and one Y-chromosome

Egg cells have 23 chromosomes only

Passing on genes

Sperm cells have 23 chromosomes only. The cells carry either an X-chromosome or a Y-chromosome, not both.

Fertilized zygote (46 chromosomes)

Embryo (46 chromosomes)

A copy of each parent's genes is passed on to their offspring when the sperm fuses with the egg.

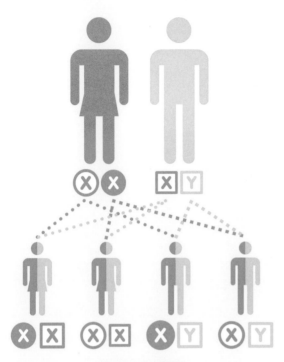

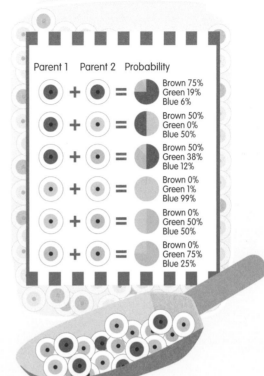

Predicting eye color

Parent 1	Parent 2	Probability
●	+ ●	= Brown 75% / Green 19% / Blue 6%
●	+ ●	= Brown 50% / Green 0% / Blue 50%
●	+ ●	= Brown 50% / Green 38% / Blue 12%
●	+ ●	= Brown 0% / Green 1% / Blue 99%
●	+ ●	= Brown 0% / Green 50% / Blue 50%
●	+ ●	= Brown 0% / Green 75% / Blue 25%

Boy or girl?

The sex of offspring is determined by whether or not the egg is fertilized by an X-carrying sperm or a Y-carrying sperm.

You have your parents' . . .

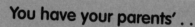

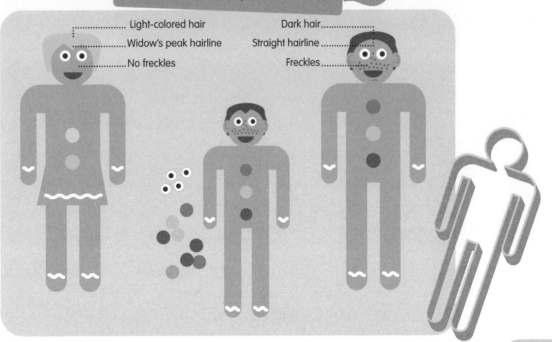

- .... Light-colored hair
- ....Widow's peak hairline
- ....No freckles
- Dark hair...................
- Straight hairline ....
- Freckles...................

This gingerbread kid has inherited the dominant traits from each of its parents. Can you spot which ones they are?

Staying healthy

The best way to keep your body in perfect condition is to take care of it. Destroy as many harmful microbes as possible before they get into your body by washing your hands regularly. Stay fit by exercising. This will also help you keep your body weight at the right level, in combination with eating a balanced diet. Always be aware of the harmful effects of the sun and protect your hearing in noisy places.

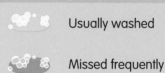

- Usually washed
- Missed frequently
- Missed most frequently

Top of hand   Underside of hand

Wash your hands well

People frequently miss certain areas of the hands while washing them. Do you clean the areas missed by others?

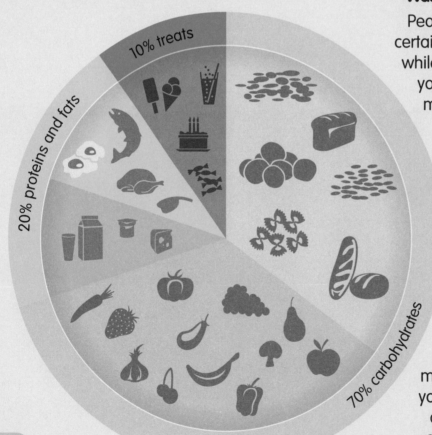

10% treats

20% proteins and fats

70% carbohydrates

Balanced diet

The sizes of these segments show how much of each type of food you should eat to maintain a balanced diet. Such a diet must contain a wide range of foods.

56

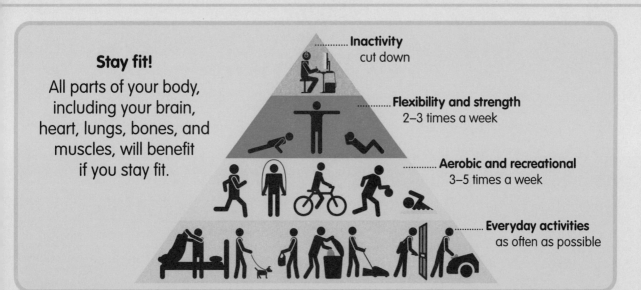

Stay fit!

All parts of your body, including your brain, heart, lungs, bones, and muscles, will benefit if you stay fit.

.... **Inactivity**
cut down

.... **Flexibility and strength**
2–3 times a week

.... **Aerobic and recreational**
3–5 times a week

.... **Everyday activities**
as often as possible

Volume control

Know how loud the sounds around you are and be aware of the maximum time that your hearing can put up with those volumes.

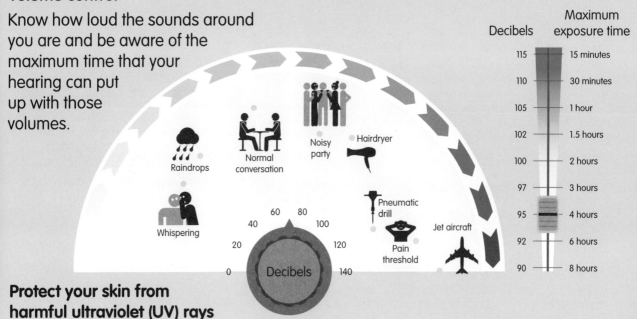

Raindrops

Normal conversation

Noisy party

Hairdryer

Whispering

Pneumatic drill

Pain threshold

Jet aircraft

Decibels

60 80
40   100
20   120
0   140

Decibels	Maximum exposure time
115	15 minutes
110	30 minutes
105	1 hour
102	1.5 hours
100	2 hours
97	3 hours
95	4 hours
92	6 hours
90	8 hours

Protect your skin from harmful ultraviolet (UV) rays

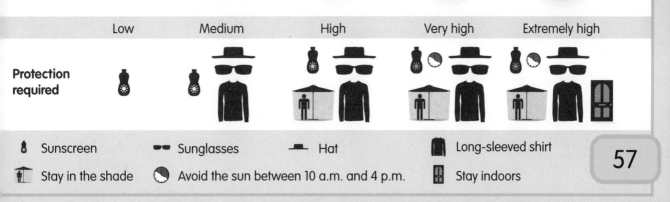

UV intensity of the sun

Low   Medium   High   Very high   Extremely high

Protection required

- Sunscreen
- Sunglasses
- Hat
- Long-sleeved shirt
- Stay in the shade
- Avoid the sun between 10 a.m. and 4 p.m.
- Stay indoors

57

Useful charts

Recommended daily amount of calories

Age	Male	Female
0 to 3 months	545	515
4 to 6 months	690	645
7 to 9 months	825	765
10 to 12 months	920	865
1 to 3 years	1,230	1,165
4 to 6 years	1,715	1,545
7 to 10 years	1,970	1,740
11 to 14 years	2,220	1,845
15 to 18 years	2,755	2,110
19 to 50 years	2,550	1,940
51 to 59 years	2,550	1,900
60 to 64 years	2,380	1,900
65 to 74 years	2,330	1,900
75+ years	2,100	1,810

Blood types

Blood types are identified by the presence, or absence, of chemical markers: A or B agglutinogen. The types can also be RhD positive or negative, so your blood can be one of eight types.

Marker on red blood cell	RhD	Blood type
none	negative	O negative
none	positive	O positive
A	negative	A negative
A	positive	A positive
B	negative	B negative
B	positive	B positive
A and B	negative	AB negative
A and B	positive	AB positive

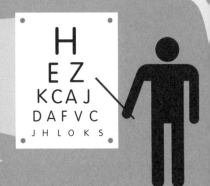

20 ft. (6m)

20/20 vision

If you have 20/20, or normal vision, you can see the letters on an eye test chart clearly from a distance of 20 ft. (6m).

Hearing frequency range

Animal	Range of hearing frequency in hertz (Hz)
Elephant	below 20
Whale	10–20
Cockroach	100–3,000
Bird	20–15,000
Human	20–20,000
Tiger	10–25,000
Dog	67–45,000
Cat	45–65,000
Bat	2,000–120,000

Calculate your sweat rate

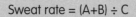

Sweat rate = (A+B) ÷ C

A = body weight before exercise – body weight after exercise

B = fluid consumed during exercise

C = amount of time spent exercising

Cold or flu?

Symptom	Cold	Flu
Fever	Sometimes	Above 100°F (38°C) for 2 days
Headaches	Rare	Common
Muscle aches	Mild	Usual, and often severe
Tiredness/weakness	Mild	Can last 2 or more weeks
Extreme exhaustion	Never	Usual
Stuffy nose/sneezing	Often	Sometimes
Sore throat	Often	Sometimes
Cough	Mild	Usual, and can be severe

Glossary

antibodies
Chemicals, released by white blood cells, that target a specific disease-causing organism and mark it for destruction.

artery
A blood vessel that carries blood away from the heart.

bacteria
A group of single-celled organisms, some of which cause disease.

bases
Four substances—adenine, cytosine, guanine, and thymine—that combine to give instructions in molecules of DNA.

bone marrow
Tissue inside bones. Some of it produces new red and white blood cells.

carbohydrate
One of the main components of food. It is broken down in the body to provide energy, partly in the form of glucose.

cell
The basic unit of all living things. A cell is capable of reproducing itself exactly.

DNA (deoxyribonucleic acid)
Molecules that carry the genetic material of living organisms.

enzyme
A substance produced by the body that helps speed up the rate of chemical reactions in the body.

frequency
The number of sound waves to pass a point in one second. Frequency is measured in units called hertz (Hz).

gene
One of about 20,000 instructions for making and running the human body. Genes are found in DNA molecules.

lymphatic vessels
A network of vessels that carries white blood cells in fluid, called lymph, to the organs of the body's defense system.

microbes
Tiny living things visible only under a microscope. Microbes include bacteria, viruses, fungi, protozoa, and algae.

molecule
A chemical unit composed of two or more linked particles called atoms.

neurons
Nerve cells that carry electrical signals through the nervous system.

nucleus
A cell's control center. It contains DNA.

nutrient
A substance, such as a carbohydrate, vitamin, or protein, needed by your body to work properly and keep you alive. You get nutrients from your food and drink.

organ
A part of the body composed of a collection of tissues. Organs are responsible for a particular function. The heart, lungs, liver, and spleen are examples of organs in your body.

organelle
One of a number of tiny structures in a cell. Each one has a specific job to do.

plasma
The liquid part of blood. Plasma contains many dissolved substances.

platelets
Disk-shaped cells that are present in large numbers in the blood. They help the blood clot and form scabs.

protein
A molecule that supplies amino acids to the body and that forms the basis of other substances, such as antibodies.

reflex
An automatic and immediate response by the body. Reflex actions usually protect the body from danger or injury.

REM (rapid eye movement) sleep
The stage of sleep during which the eyeballs are constantly moving.

saliva
A watery fluid, released by glands in the mouth, that helps you chew, taste, and digest your food.

sweat rate
The amount of fluid you lose during each hour of exercise under your normal exercise conditions.

tissue
A group of one type (or similar types) of cells, which work together to perform a particular function. Tissues combine to form an organ.

vein
A vessel that carries blood to the heart.

virus
A microscopic organism that infects and destroys body cells so that it may reproduce itself.

vitamins
A group of substances in food that are vital in tiny amounts for healthy growth.

zygote
The cell produced when an egg is fertilized by the sperm.

Index

Find out more

 Books to read

Everything You Need to Know about the Human Body by Patricia Macnair (Kingfisher, 2011)
Human Body Factory by Dan Green (Kingfisher, 2012)
Human Body (Discovery Explore Your World) by Steve Parker (DK Adult, 2007)
The Usborne Complete Book of the Human Body by Anna Claybourne (Usborne, 2004)
Wow! Human Body by Richard Walker (DK, 2010)

 Websites to visit

Look closely at blood:
www.e-learningforkids.org/Courses/Liquid_Animation/Body_Parts/Blood/index.html

Watch this movie to see how the digestive system works:
http://kidshealth.org/kid/htbw/DSmovie.html

Find out how your body's defense system acts like a castle:
www.cyh.com/HealthTopics/HealthTopicDetailsKids.aspx?p=335&np=152&id=2402

 Places to visit

Take a walking tour through the human body at the Health Museum's Amazing
Human Body Pavilion:
Hermann Drive, Houston, TX 77004
Phone: (713) 521-1515
www.mhms.org

Discover "You: the Experience": one of the first and largest exhibitions showcasing
the connection between the human mind, body, and spirit in the 21st century, at the
Museum of Science and Industry:
South Lake Shore Drive, Chicago, IL 60637
Phone: (773) 684-1414
www.msichicago.org

Visit the National Geographic Museum and see adventures and
scientific research come to life:
17th Street Northwest, Washington, D.C. 20036
Phone: (202) 857-7588
www.nationalgeographic.com